Bruce Tegner has devised a completely modern adaptation of classic European and traditional Asian styles of stick-fighting using articles which are widely available and which are commonly carried by many people.

The defenses can be learned easily and they can be remembered without constant practice. They are appropriate for men and women in today's world. Included is a section on self-defense for the blind and other physically disabled individuals. There is a special section of baton techniques for security officers.

Bruce Tegner's approach to the subject is realistic and ethical. He does not resort to vicious counter-violence. He selects and teaches techniques which give maximum protection and enhance self-confidence using the least force possible for effective self-defense.

STICK FIGHTING: SELF-DEFENSE

by

BRUCE TEGNER

THOR PUBLISHING COMPANY

VENTURA, CALIFORNIA 93001

Catalog Information

TEGNER, BRUCE

   Stick fighting: self-defense

   1. Stick fighting   I. Title
GV1141.T42   796.8   70-109225
ISBN 0-87407-020-1   MARC

STICK-FIGHTING: SELF-DEFENSE

Printing History:

First edition: June 1972
Second printing: July 1973
Third printing: August 1974
Fourth printing: January 1976
Fifth printing: March 1979

Manuscript prepared under the supervision of ALICE McGRATH

THOR PUBLISHING COMPANY
P.O. BOX 1782
VENTURA, CA 93001

BRUCE TEGNER BOOKS REVIEWED

BRUCE TEGNER'S COMPLETE BOOK OF SELF-DEFENSE
Recommended for Y.A. in the American Library Association
BOOKLIST

BRUCE TEGNER'S COMPLETE BOOK OF JUDO
"...the definitive text...ideal for instructors and individuals."
SCHOLASTIC COACH

BRUCE TEGNER'S COMPLETE BOOK OF JUJITSU
"...authoritative and easy-to-follow text...clear photos."
SCHOOL LIBRARY JOURNAL

KARATE: Self-defense & Traditional Forms
Recommended for Y.A. in the American Library Association
BOOKLIST

BRUCE TEGNER'S COMPLETE BOOK OF KARATE
"Tegner suggests and illustrates changes to bring karate in
line with modern concepts of physical education...invaluable
for teaching karate in schools, colleges and recreation centers."
CAPHER

SELF-DEFENSE FOR YOUR CHILD (with Alice McGrath)
[For elementary school age boys & girls]
    "...informative, readable book for family use..."
CHRISTIAN HOME & SCHOOL

    "...intelligent, clear-headed approach..."   BOOKS WEST

SELF-DEFENSE & ASSAULT PREVENTION FOR GIRLS & WOMEN (with
Alice McGrath)
"...should be required reading for all girls and women..."
WILSON LIBRARY BULLETIN
"...simple and straightforward with no condescension...easy to
learn and viable as defense tactics..."   SCHOOL LIBRARY JOURNAL

BRUCE TEGNER'S COMPLETE BOOK OF JUKADO
"This is the most useful book on the Oriental fighting arts I
have ever seen."   LIBRARY JOURNAL

SELF-DEFENSE NERVE CENTERS & PRESSURE POINTS
"Students and teachers will find much valuable source
material in this attractive book."   SCHOLASTIC COACH

SELF-DEFENSE FOR BOYS & MEN: A Physical Education Course
"...recommended for school libraries. The text deserves
. inspection by P.E. instructors."   LIBRARY JOURNAL

KUNG FU & TAI CHI: Chinese Karate and Classical Exercise
"...recommended for physical fitness collections."
LIBRARY JOURNAL

CONTENTS

For demonstrating the techniques with him
in the photos, the author is grateful to
JEAN WINDISHAR, RICHARD WINDISHAR,
JACK GRUEL and NEIL ZIEGLER.

To the UNCLE SAM UMBRELLA SHOP in New
York City, the author wishes to extend thanks for
many courtesies extended during the preparation of
this book.

INTRODUCTION

STICK DEFENSE: When & Why

The use of sticks for self-defense has a long history. There is evidence that prehistoric man used sticks for his first tools and as his first weapons.

Since then, man has devised both tools and weapons which are infinitely more sophisticated. Still, there are occasions in which a handy stick is used with success as an improvised tool--and as an improvised weapon. This book is intended to teach you to use a stick for self-defense, without using it in a needlessly violent way. In spite of the amount of violence present in our society, most people ardently wish for a decrease in violence. The problem arises, in a situation where fear of violence is widespread, how does one manage to feel adequately protected without contributing to the total sum of violence in the society?

There is more than enough proof that carrying guns for "self-defense" aggravates the very problem it is supposed to cope with. Few criminals are shot in self-defense; most people killed in gun shootings are innocent, accidental victims.

Even if this were not true, most people are not willing to use guns, even in self-defense. Though a stick is a weapon, it does not have the same connotation of deadly violence as does a gun or cutting weapon. Although there is the possibility that a stick could be used in a bludgeoning, offensive manner, it can also be used for protection without the brutal consequences inherent in a gun.

SPORT & SELF-DEFENSE: The Difference

Sport and ceremonial forms of stick fighting are not suitable for modern street defense. The goals, the selection of material, the level of technical skill and the manner of training are different for sport forms of stick fighting than they are for practical self-defense.

Basic stick fighting defenses, if they are to be of value to those who need them the most, must be simple and easy to learn; they must not require intensive, on-going practice; they should not rely on peak physical fitness.

For sport forms of stick fighting, as for contest forms of any physical skill, a high degree of technical excellence and peak physical condition are essential. Neither technical skill nor physical condition can be maintained without rigorous, continuing training and practice.

In contest, the object is to demonstrate style and technique and a necessary condition of engaging in contest is endurance. In a defense situation, subtle style of technique is irrelevant; the object is to avoid getting hurt, to stop the assailant as quickly as possible and to escape. The defense must be carried on for as long as necessary, but it must not be prolonged for longer than necessary.

Complicated and difficult-to-learn techniques have no place in a course of modern defense for practical use. Few individuals can learn the complicated techniques; without constant on-going practice the complicated defenses are forgotten.

A complete repertoire of stick defense tactics does not involve learning a great number of techniques. Having a basic repertoire of stick defenses involves learning a relatively small group of tactics and knowing how to use them in a flexible and functional manner. The old-fashioned method of teaching Asian styles of stick fighting proceeds on the assumption that a separate defense must be learned for each attack. This requires learning hundreds of separate "tricks" or attack/ defense sequences, many of which are not realistic in this century; they are merely traditional vestiges of an ancient sword-carrying and staff-carrying time. The traditional stick fighting techniques are wonderful for recreation, physical fitness and sport, but they must not be confused with stick fighting for modern self-defense.

DON'T DEPEND ON THE STICK

Using a stick for self-defense is a way of making the defense more efficient. The stick defenses can be used effectively without needless violence. However, the stick should not, except in the instances noted below, be considered the defense of first choice. If you are in normal good health and have the functional use of your limbs, you should learn weaponless self-defense and think of the stick defenses as backup techniques.

Total reliance on the stick weapon leads to a feeling of helplessness if the stick is not available or is taken away from you. Most individuals can learn weaponless defense for most of the situations they would ever encounter.

The exceptions are, of course, individuals who are more than normally frail, those who have an orthopedic disability and those who live or work under more than ordinarily hazardous conditions. Even such individuals should learn as much as possible of weaponless self-defense so that they can avoid total dependence on the stick weapon.

Being prepared to cope with possible assault will give you the poise necessary to face such a threat without paralyzing panic. When you have greater confidence to cope with possible assault you have greater self-control and, therefore, greater control of the threatening situation. Many assaults take place under circumstances in which the victim has unwittingly made himself (or herself) vulnerable to the assault.

Minimizing the possibility of assault is as much a part of practical defense as is learning the physical techniques. It is not necessary to live in paranoid fear to reduce the possibility that you might be the victim of assault; exercising ordinary prudence will protect you from the most common attacks. Few assaults take place on well-lighted, well-traveled streets; they occur in dark, unpopulated areas, short-cuts, alleys and by-ways. Everyone should know the rules of safety on the street. If you do not know what they are, find out from your local police. Then put them into practice.

WHICH STICKS FOR SELF-DEFENSE?

Because this is essentially a manual for the use of the non-specialist, non-professional person, I have chosen to demonstrate the defenses with only those sticks which such individuals are likely to have available and only those sticks with which modern street defenses are practical.

Sport forms of stick fighting are not included in this volume for the reasons given earlier and therefore the sticks for sport fighting are not shown. For instance the long stick or staff, which was commonly carried by travelers in medieval times, is not appropriate for self-defense today. It is as impractical to teach staff defenses for modern use as it would be to teach archery for self-defense. Fencing and sword fighting were once commonplace for hand-to-hand combat; they are now archaic with respect to their original uses, but they have become excellent forms of exercise and recreation. The ancient forms of staff fighting can be converted into enjoyable physical fitness and recreation activities but they should not be confused with basic, useful self-defense.

USE THE ENTIRE BOOK

For the maximum amount of instruction and information from this book, it is suggested that you read the entire book, whether or not you have an interest in the various special uses for the different types of sticks. It would have been needlessly repetitious to have given defense examples for each specific stick in each of the sections. Make adaptations of appropriate material from all the sections taking into account your own personal needs, requirements and preferences.

NOMENCLATURE

Whether you are using a cane, umbrella, walking stick or improvised stick weapon, the references to the parts of the stick will be the same. Although strictly speaking some sticks do not have a handle, the way the stick is carried will determine which end is the point and which the handle.

1. The end of the stick which you hold is the handle or butt.

2. The end opposite the butt is the point.

3. The portion between your hand grips is the middle.

PRACTICE: Level of Skill

The amount of practice, the method of practice and the level of skill to be reached will vary considerably from individual to individual. Minimum preparation to avoid the role of helpless victim does not require high skill or rigorous training and practice.

Basic skill could be reached by reading the relevant material and shadow-practicing it to rehearse the gestures and movements. Working with a partner will allow you to achieve a higher level of skill. Those who wish to reach the highest potential of stick defense skill will have to work hard, train regularly and maintain technical skill with on-going practice.

BALANCE & T-POSITION

4. Standing as shown, in a relaxed position, a person is in very weak balance.

5. If you experiment, you will find that fingertip pressure is enough to break balance backward.

6. Grasping cloth with your fingertips and pulling forward is enough to break balance forward.

7. The T-position, the stance of the fencer, is the strongest balance possible on two points--that is, standing on both feet. If you try it, you will discover that the person who was so easy to pull or push off balance from the relaxed position is not so easy to push or pull off balance when he is in the T-position. This is the favored stance for defense and you should, in practice, assume the T-stance whenever you can. If you step into T-position during practice, you can develop the habit of taking this strong balance automatically.

8. The weakest position is on one point--that is, standing on one foot. From this position you are even more vulnerable than in the two-point position.

9. Three-point balance can be assumed by placing the cane or umbrella so that both feet and the point of the cane form a triangle.

4

5

6

7

8

9

SAFETY IN PRACTICE

If you work with a partner, observe safety rules carefully. Getting hit with a stick is painful and it is not necessary to endure pain to learn stick self-defense. Touching lightly at the body targets is sufficient realism for stick work. If you wish to make light contact blows on each other, pad your arms and legs with some kind of protective material. Practice partners should never make full-force contact blows on each other. If you need to practice full-force blows, use a practice dummy or improvise a hitting surface which you can strike without danger of damage.

LEFT & RIGHT

Although the techniques are shown on one side only, repeat them on the other side as well. Basic tactics should be practiced with right and left hand. Defenses should be practiced to the right and left sides. Do not rely too heavily on your lead hand. If you are right-handed, emphasize the left hand in practice. If you are left-handed, emphasize the right hand in practice.

DEADLY DEFENSE?

There are some very important reasons why self-defense must and ought to involve the least possible use of force. The legal limits on self-defense are clear: You may use that amount of force which is necessary for your own protection; you may not use unnecessary force or inflict unnecessary injury. The only way to be certain of avoiding unnecessary injury is to avoid using tactics which involve a high risk of injury. There are alternate tactics which are very effective for self-defense without the high risk of injury.

Traditional styles of Asian weaponless and stick fighting often treat all assaults as though they were deadly and teach "defenses" which are more vicious than the assault. Preparation in modern defense techniques should involve the knowledge of the legal and ethical restraints on the use of force. If an individual kills an assailant, even in self-defense, he is responsible for his actions. He must offer convincing proof that he was not to blame for having started the fight. The man who picks up a bludgeon and fatally injures someone in an argument may plead self-defense. The plea alone is not enough; there must be evidence.

So there is a legal boundary on "deadly" defense. There is a second consideration, one which would operate even in the absence of the law. If you inflict fatal injury, you must live the rest of your life with the consequences of that act. A decent human being finds it a heavy burden.

It is for the reasons outlined above, the second as much as the first, that I have omitted tactics and targets which involve the highest risk of serious permanent injury or fatality.

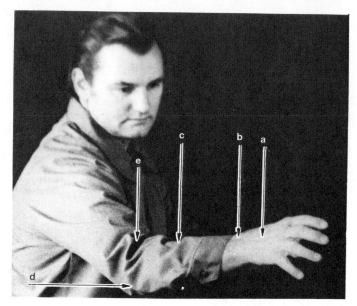

10

BODY TARGETS

PHOTO 10. Many hostile or assaultive actions begin with a reaching arm. Hitting at the arm or hand to stop or deflect the assault is an effective defense.

a. Onto the Hand. It is possible to hit onto the back of the hand to deflect it without coming into fist range of the assailant.

b. Onto the Wrist. Hitting onto the wrist has about the same effect as hitting at the hand.

c. Onto the Forearm. At the mound of the forearm there is a concentration of nerves. Hitting at this area can numb the arm briefly.

d. Elbow. Hitting onto the point of the elbow causes pain.

e. Bend of the Elbow. Hitting into the bend of the elbow causes pain and bends the arm, deflecting it.

PHOTO 11.

a. Onto the Shoulder Muscle. Striking at the base of the neck, on the top of the shoulder, can numb and temporarily disable the arm.

b. Side of the Neck. Hitting into the side of the neck is effective, but not vicious. Unlike hitting into the windpipe, which is a very high risk tactic, a stick blow into the side of the neck results in considerable pain and could cause unconsciousness, but there is little likelihood of serious or fatal injury unless an extremely forceful blow is delivered at great speed.

c. Mid-body. A jabbing blow into the fleshy mid-body area causes considerable pain. An extremely forceful blow made with great speed could cause internal injury.

d. Groin. Hitting into the groin has limited use. There is a fast, almost automatic response to protect the groin. It is imprudent to step in close to the assailant to deliver a knee kick to the groin if you can conduct your defense from out of his fist range. But with a long stick weapon, such as a cane or umbrella, you can hit into the groin with an upward whipping action, or you can hit *toward* the groin as a diversionary tactic.

e. Knee. A snappy blow to the side of the knee causes pain. A forceful blow could buckle the knee, possibly sprain it, possibly put him on the ground.

f. Shin. Most individuals are particularly sensitive at the shin, where little flesh protects the nerves. It would require an extremely forceful blow by a strong person to cause fracture, but even a small individual can hit at this area and effect considerable pain and disorientation.

g. Ankle/Foot. Hitting at the ankle is effective for the particular situations when it is appropriate. Defending from the ground the ankle is a good target. Against a toe kick, hitting the ankle or foot is expedient.

From the rear, the target areas are: Side of the neck; arms and hands, if extended; back of the knee; ankles.

For most instances of self-defense it is not necessary to hit into the head. A stick blow into the head involves high risk of injury. (Certain exceptions are noted in the section on the hand stick.) It is possible to use stick blows *toward* the face as excellent diversionary tactics. If you feint a stick blow to the face, there is a drawing-back response.

HAND & FOOT BLOWS

Total dependence on the stick weapon is neither prudent nor practical. Unless you have a disability or dysfunction which prevents it, you should learn a few techniques of hitting and kicking which can be used in conjunction with the stick defenses.

HAND BLOWS

The single most versatile, practical, effective open-hand blow is made with the outside edge of the hand, using a choppy, slashing action. Originally known as the judo or jujitsu chop, this blow is commonly referred to as the karate chop or kung fu chop.

Hit with the fleshy part of the edge of the palm. Avoid hitting onto the bones of the little finger or the wrist. Your thumb is held alongside your index finger. Your hand is slightly cupped and held firm but not rigid.

The targets are:

12. Onto the hand or wrist.

13. Onto the forearm.

14. Into the elbow.

15. Into the side of the neck.

12

13

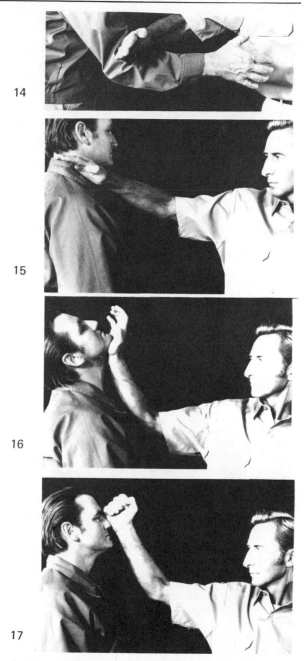

14

15

16

17

16. The heel-of-palm blow is made by bending your wrist back sharply, and curling your fingers so that you do not use them for hitting. The target is up under the jaw or nose.

17. Hitting with the side of the fist onto the nose is effective and easy.

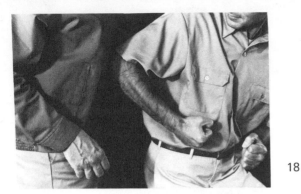

18

18. Hitting at an assailant behind you, strike with the point of the elbow.

KICKING

The combination of kicking and stick blows is highly effective. You need learn only a few basic kicks for self-defense. These are the most practical kicks. They are relatively easy to learn and they can be remembered for use without constant practice.

19

19. Using the outside edge of your shoe as the striking point, snap out sharply, aiming at the shin area as your target. Practice to deliver this kick as a fast, flicking snap. Hit with the middle of the edge of the shoe for the most effective kick.

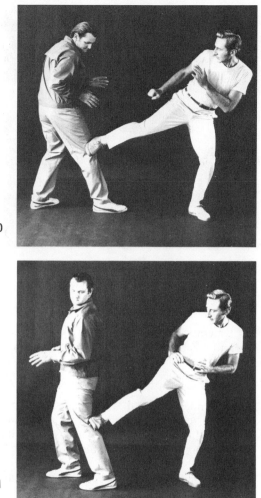

20

21

20. With the center of the bottom of your shoe, kick into the knee area, using a stamping, thrusting action.

Hitting with the heel delivers effective force, but requires more accuracy. If you practice kicking with the middle of the bottom of your shoe, you have some leeway for error. Practice by drawing your kicking leg up, with your knee bent sharply, then stamp out vigorously.

21. Practice kicking with the bottom of your shoe into the back of the knee of the assailant. If you move around to the side or rear, a single vigorous kick into the back of the knee could buckle him down or put him in awkward balance.

22

22. Against an assailant behind you, you can use the bottom-of-the-shoe kick to the rear, hitting into the knee.

23. Or you could use the snap kick to the shin with the edge of your shoe. In practicing kicks to the rear, look at your target as you kick.

24. Using the edge of your shoe, scrape down the shin . . .

25. . . . and complete the action by stamping down onto the top of his foot. The scraping, stamping combination is effective and practical for those situations when you are already close in to the assailant. Do not step in close to apply this combination.

When practicing the kicks, maintain good balance as you recover.

Both the bottom-of-the-shoe and edge-of-the-shoe kicks can be delivered from out of fist range of the assailant and both kicks can be used effectively by a smaller individual against a considerably larger assailant.

Avoid the error of stepping in unnecessarily close to the assailant to deliver kicks. There is a common tendency to step in as a blow is delivered. You can overcome this tendency in practice by taking a step back before you kick.

23

24

25

CANE, UMBRELLA, WALKING STICK

The cane, umbrella and walking stick are ideal for self-defense. Without appearing conspicuous or out of the ordinary, you can carry a cane or walking stick at any time. An umbrella can be substituted for the cane or walking stick when weather and other conditions are appropriate.

There are many kinds of canes, umbrellas and walking sticks available, from the most expensive, ornamental styles to the least expensive, purely functional types.

You should get into the habit of carrying your stick with you so that you are comfortable and relaxed with it.

Practice the defenses using the stick you will actually carry. The defenses which are shown for cane, umbrella and walking stick may also be used with improvised sticks such as broom or mop or the wand of a vacuum cleaner.

ONE HAND GRIPS & USES

The normal way of carrying a cane, umbrella or walking stick is with one hand. The first method of striking which you will practice utilizes this most common grip, preparing you to use a defense from the normal carrying position.

These striking areas are available for most situations. They are the practical self-defense targets.

26. Holding the stick in the one-handed grip, strike with a whipping action. Hit onto the back of the hand.

27. Hit the wrist with a whipping action. Hitting into the palm is ineffective, but hitting the wrist from any angle is an effective action.

28. Whip down onto the forearm. You can also hit into the bend of the elbow, the elbow joint or the muscle areas of the outside of the arm. (See section on body target areas.)

29. Using a whipping action, slash into the side of the neck.

30. A whipping, slashing action into the knee.

31. Across the shin bone, a snappy blow is effective.

26

27

28

29

30

31

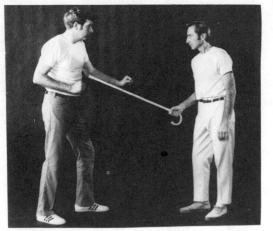

32

Jabbing Blows

The jabbing blow can be delivered with the stick held at the handle end or at the middle. Hitting a jabbing blow with a mid-grip gives greater force and thrust, but you should also practice the jabbing blows from the normal, handle-held position. The action is a fast, stabbing thrust.

The target area for jabbing blows is mid-body, into the solar plexus, stomach or abdomen.

32. Using the ordinary walking stick grip, jab into the solar plexus without changing your hand position.

33, 34. Holding the stick at the middle, deliver a stabbing blow into the mid-section.

33   34

35

36

Point Grip

The point grip is not a common way of carrying a stick, but you should be able to deliver blows using a point grip if that is how you happen to pick it up.

35. First, deliver a short, jabbing blow into the mid-section with the point of the stick.

36. Follow the jabbing blow with a whipping, circular action, hitting with the handle end of the stick into the side of the neck.

Against a serious, close-in assault, it would be possible to use the point, raking it back and forth against the assailant's face.

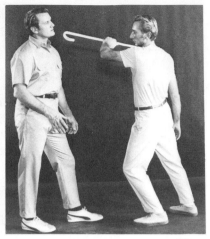

37

38

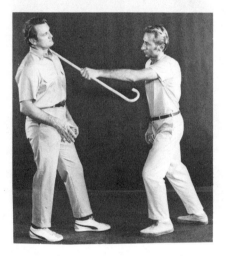

39

One-Handed Middle Grip

In this sequence of blows the striking point alternates between the point end and the handle.

37. Hold the stick at the middle. Begin the sequence with a point blow forward into the solar plexus.

38. Follow the first blow with an upward raking blow under the chin. Follow the raking blow with a smashing forward blow, using the handle for striking.

39. The fourth blow is a whipping action into the side of the neck, using the point end for striking.

40

41

TWO-HANDED GRIPS & USES

The two methods of holding two-handed are: A. Grip the stick with both hands palm down. B. Grip the stick with one hand palm up and the other hand palm down. Practice all the two-handed techniques using both these grips and select for your own use those which seem most comfortable for you and which you prefer.

Block/Parry

Because so many assaults begin with a reaching action, practice blocking and deflecting the reaching arms (or arm) first.

40. With a firm, two-handed grip on the stick, strike downward onto the forearm.

41. As the reaching arms come forward, block upward, deflecting his arms up.

42

42. As the reaching arms come forward, take a step to the side and thrust his arms away, as shown.

Two-Handed Thrust

To deliver the most efficient blow, hold the stick about six inches from each end. The action is a thrust with follow-through. This is exactly the same action as is used for blocking/deflecting, but now it is applied as a hitting blow.

43. Hit straight forward toward the upper chest to push him away and put him into awkward balance.

44. Hit up under the chin.

45. Hit down onto the nose.

Two-Handed Jabbing

Two-handed jabbing blows can be delivered with point or handle. Blows delivered with the point end have greater penetration power, but be prepared to strike with either end.

46. Additional force can be given to a jabbing blow by taking a step as you strike. The blow shown here is being made with the point end.

47. The handle can be used for a jabbing blow to the rear, as shown, or it can be used to strike forward.

43

44

45

46

47

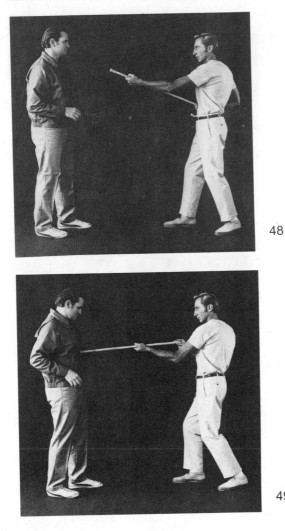

48

49

Cue-Shot Jab

The action of this blow is similar to that of a cue shot.

48. The stick is gripped firmly at the handle end and the point end is held loosely, palm up.

49. Driving with your right hand, thrust the stick through your left hand and deliver a stabbing, jabbing blow with recoil action.

Hit into the midsection or toward the face.

50   51

Two-Handed Blow: From One Hand Grip

Practice holding the stick with one hand, in the normal carrying position, and as you raise it for use, grip with the other hand to give additional force to the blow.

50. From the normal one-handed grip on the cane, as you raise it, grip with the other hand and strike into the side of the neck, or down onto the shoulder muscle.

51. Follow the first blow with a second into the other side of the neck.

Practice the combination of two blows using this grip and aim at the other body targets.

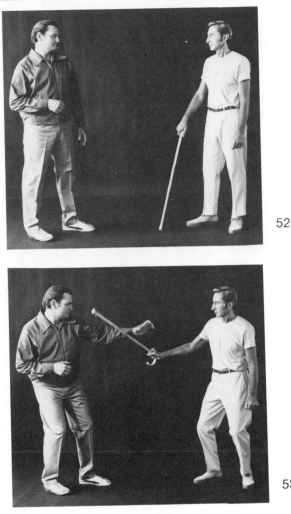

52

53

ALERT POSITIONS

There are a number of positions which allow you to move quickly for defense if necessary. Depending on the situation, you might prefer to present a casual appearance or you might wish to indicate that you are aware of possible threat of assault.

52. Holding the stick slightly in front of you, standing in a modified T-position for strong balance, you are prepared to hit, if necessary, but your appearance is neutral, non-aggressive, non-hostile.

53. Without changing your hand position, you can hit quickly up under the chin or up against a reaching arm.

54

55

54. If your demeanor is appropriately calm and neutral, you can hold your stick ready for use two-handed, without giving the impression of hostility. A modified T-position gives you strong balance.

55. You can strike at the reaching arm . . .

56

56 . . . or you can use the cue-stick blow into the mid-body.

SPRING TENSION BLOW

57. In an alert position, hold the stick as shown, gripping the
handle end with your right hand holding the point end of the
stick with your left hand. The tension is created by holding the
point end lightly and by pushing forward with your right thumb
as you pull back with the fingers of your right hand. The action
is somewhat like bowing a flexible stick.

58. As he moves in, strike into the side of the neck with a
whipping blow which is given added force by the spring tension.

59. To deliver a tension blow using the handle end for striking,
hold the stick in both hands, gripping lightly with your right
hand and creating the spring action by pushing with your left
thumb and pulling back with the fingers of your left hand.

60. If necessary, you can move quickly, using the handle end of
the stick for striking.

57

58

59

60

FLEXIBLE WALKING STICK

A very light, flexible walking stick can be used to deliver the blows which have been shown with cane, umbrella and other rigid sticks. The flexible stick can also be used in the following manner:

61. Spring tension is created by bowing back on the stick slightly at both ends. The striking point of the flexible stick is either the knob (handle) or the point. Hitting with the knob delivers a more forceful blow; hitting with the point end delivers a sharper, stinging blow.

62. You can deliver a sharp, stinging blow into the side of the neck.

63. Or, you can deliver a whipping action blow into the shin.

64. In this example, the knob end is used for striking. The spring tension gives added snap to the blow.

65. The target area could be onto the arm or into the side of the neck.

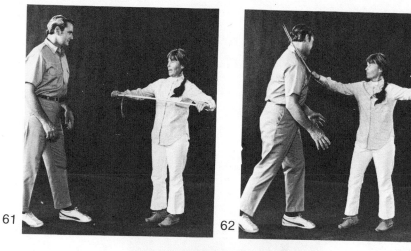

61

62

63

64

65

RELEASING GRABBED STICK

One-Handed Grip

66. Your stick is grabbed with one hand.

67. Do not pull the stick away from him; if his grip is strong you will not be able to wrestle it out. Kick into the shin.

68. Hit him with the end of the cane which he is not gripping.

If this does not effect release, kick him again as you twist the held end sharply in a circle.

66

67

68

Two-Handed Grip

69. Kick sharply into the shin.

70. Scrape down the shin and stamp onto his foot.

71. Do not attempt to pull away. Twist the stick in a circular motion, sharply.

72. Hit into the side of the head or neck.

If the first twisting action does not effect release, kick again, with vigor and twist in the opposite direction.

69

70

71

72

DEFLECTING KICKS

Trying to grip or grapple with a kicking leg is difficult and inefficient. Your best defense, if you cannot move out of range, is deflecting the kick.

Practice one-handed and two-handed deflection actions. Practice as though deflecting a toe kick and practice to deflect a knee kick.

73

74

73. With a sharp, whipping action, hit the kicking leg; use follow-through to deflect the intended kick as much as possible.

74. With a two-handed grip (which gives greater force to your stick blow) deflect the knee kick.

Practice deflecting kicks made with right foot and with left foot.

RISING FROM GROUND

If you have fallen or been pushed to the ground, use the cane as a flailing or jabbing instrument as you arise. If you do not keep the cane moving, you are especially vulnerable while you are getting up.

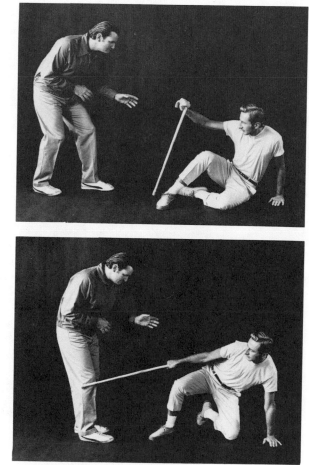

75

76

75. Keep your head away from your assailant. Do not move toward him as you get up; scoot back away from him if you can.

76. Keeping the cane in motion, rise facing him and be prepared to use stick and foot blows, if necessary.

COMBINING ACTIONS

A few techniques, applied in a spirited and determined manner, can be used to cope with most of the intended assaults most people would ever encounter. The procedures which follow are for learning to combine the stick blows in the most flexible and versatile way.

The practice procedures will start with the combination of two blows and will take you through combinations which simulate defenses against the most common assault attempts.

One-Two Combination

After practicing the separate stick blows of the foregoing instruction, practice combinations to simulate an on-going defense.

An on-going defense could be the repetition of a single blow, for as long as necessary. A more sophisticated defense would be the combination of a variety of blows. Utilizing the different styles of blows makes your defense more effective.

Make one-two combinations of all the blows you have learned; combine them in all the possible variations you can think of. When you begin this procedure, you need not be concerned with speed, but practice for smooth, flowing actions without hesitation between the two blows. Then, practice to deliver the two blows in quick succession.

77   78

Start from an alert position, holding the stick in the normal way.

77. Strike a snappy blow onto the forearm.

78. Without hesitation, follow the first blow with a whipping blow into the side of the neck.

Practice two different blows in succession. Practice two others, until you have gone through all the blows, one-handed and two-handed. Practice all of the one-handed blows using your right hand and then your left hand for striking the first blow.

When you can deliver two successive blows with functional skill, you will advance to delivering four blows in succession. Examples of four-blow combinations follow. These little routines may be practiced briefly to acquaint you with the concept of four techniques combined in a continuous sequence.

In the solo sequences, reference is to an imaginary opponent. Visualize the target area.

Four One-Handed Blows

79. Holding the cane at the handle, strike up.

80. Without hesitation, hit into his left side with a circular whipping blow.

81. Without hesitation, strike downward, onto the shoulder.

82. Finish the sequence with a back-handed blow into the leg.

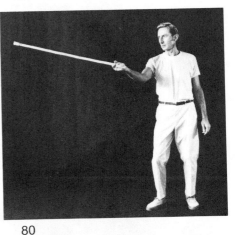

79   80

81   82

Block & Hit Combinations

Practice combining the two-handed blocking action with other defense techniques. Shown here are only two of many possible combinations.

83. As you block the reaching arm, kick with vigor into the shin.

84. Another possible combination begins with a downward thrusting block against the reaching arms.

85. The downward block is immediately followed by an upward thrust under the chin.

Practice many combinations of the various blocking actions followed by a second defense action using a kick or a two-handed blow.

83

84

85

Four Two-Handed Blows

86. Holding the cane with both hands, jab forward with the point as you take a short step with your left foot.

87. Step forward with your right foot as you hit upward with the handle.

88. Thrust forward with the handle. (no foot movement)

89. Step forward with your left foot as you hit over and down with the point end.

86

87

88

89

Five-Blow Sequence

90. Start from a relaxed standing position, point of cane on the floor.

91. Grip the handle end with your left hand and deliver a blow into the side.

92. Deliver a back-handed, whipping blow into the other side.

93. Slide your left hand to the point end of the stick as you step forward with your right foot and hit with the handle end.

90

91

92

93

94   95

94. Without foot movement, deliver a cue-stick thrust, using the handle end to strike.

95. As you take a step forward with your left foot, deliver a blow over and down with the point end of the stick.

FLEXIBLE RESPONSE

When you have practiced the material to this point in the text, and can use the stick blows (and kicks and hand blows) with a moderate (functional) degree of skill, you have already learned how to cope with many assault attempts. *Most* assault attempts can be stopped with one or two blows. Once you demonstrate your refusal to play the part of the helpless victim, you may not have to do anything more.

Following are some examples of common types of assault. The defenses could be applied with equal efficiency to many similar situations. It is intentional that only the first blow of the defense is indicated; the aim of this practice is to prepare you for flexible response, rather than to teach you rigid, prearranged sequences of actions.

Many assaults begin with a reaching forward or moving forward. You do not have to wait until the first aggressive action is completed; your best defense is based on the concept of stopping or deflecting the intended aggressive action.

ONE ARM REACHING OR PUNCHING

It is not necessary to wait for the aggressive action to be completed. The intent could be punching, poking, grabbing, pushing or pulling; you react to the reaching arm, not to the specific type of attack. What you use would depend on your preference and the relative space/position relationships.

96. A first response could be an upward blocking blow, followed by one or two additional blows of your choice.

97. An equally effective response could be a deflecting/parry blow, followed by one or two actions of your choice.

98. Or, you might choose to begin your defense with a blow into the wrist, followed by any two additional techniques you want to use.

96

97

98

99   100

99. Against two reaching arms, your defense response is to the reaching action. It is not necessary to wait to see if his intention is to push, grab, choke or pull. You could begin your defense with a two-handed upward thrust, followed by other blows of your choice.

100. Or, you could use a side block/parry as your first action.

101. Or, you could use a jabbing action to hold him off, following with two more blows of your choice.

102. Against a wrist grip, the most effective first action would be to strike against the gripping hand or wrist, following the first blow with others of your choice. You might elect to continue to hit at the gripping hand.

101

102

103

104

103. Hitting downward against two arms gripping (or grabbing or choking) is an appropriate first action, which could be followed by any two other blows of your choice.

104. Effective first action against a back shoulder-grab would be a whipping back blow; turn immediately to face the assailant and continue the defense, using two other blows of your choice.

BACK GRAB

105. Surprise back grab has been completed. Kick into the shin with vigor; repeat to hurt him and prepare for the next action.

106. Take a deep breath to expand your chest and grip the stick with both hands, as shown.

107. Exhale sharply as you bend your knees and twist your body. Hit into his mid-body and immediately step out of his fist range. If necessary, continue to hit with stick and kick as required.

105

106

107

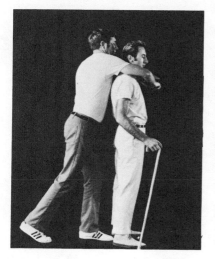 

108   109

BACK CHOKE

The essential first action of defending against an applied choke is relief from the pain and pressure. Unless you diminish the amount of pain, you cannot apply your defense effectively; unless you diminish the force of the choke, you are in danger of losing consciousness.

108. A surprise back attack; choke is applied with the forearm against your throat.

109. Grip the choking arm near the wrist and pull down sharply. This will not break the choke, but it will diminish its force. Maintaining a firm grip on the choking arm, hit back into the head with the stick. Kick with vigor into his shin. Do not let go of his choking arm as you hit and kick!

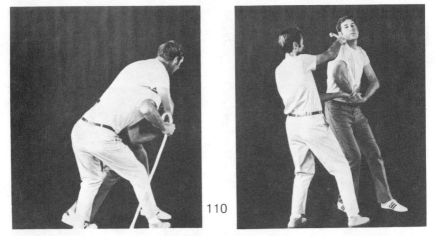

110

111

110. When you have weakened him and hurt him with kicks and blows, duck down sharply and step back and out from under his grip, still maintaining your hold on his arm.

111. If necessary, continue to hit with the stick and use kicks as required to permit your escape.

MORE THAN ONE ASSAILANT Holding-Off: Figure-8

Showing a willingness to defend and preparedness to defend in an orderly manner, might be enough to prevent an assault by two assailants. Gang attacks are not made by those who are brave, but by those who need easy victims. Your obvious intention to avoid being a willing victim could deter two assailants. The two holding-off actions shown here require only minimum practice to make them available to you as a preventive defense.

112

112. Whipping the stick in a figure-8, keep a spirited, continuous action going.

113

113. Whirling the stick around your head, keep the stick moving to deter assailants coming in from different directions.

Assault Front & Rear

114. The threat of assault is made from the front and from the back

115. Using stick and foot blows, hit at both assailants simultaneously.

114

115

116

117

116. Immediately reverse your actions to hit and kick again, in both directions.

117. Get around to the side or rear of one man and, using him as a shield, push him into the other man.

Continue the defense, if necessary, using stick blows and kicks until you can escape.

Facing

The assailants in this example are coming from the same direction. If you can evaluate which is the leader, start your defense by hitting him first.

118. Get out to the side, if you can. Make simultaneous stick and foot blows, hitting two assailants at the same time.

119. As you move around to the outside of the group, continue hitting with the stick.

120. Get around behind one man and, using him as a shield, push him into the others. If necessary, carry on the defense, continuing to hit, kick and move.

118

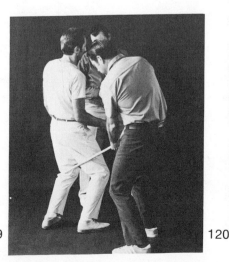

119

120

STICK AGAINST STICK

The defenses against the stick attacks shown here would also be used against attacks using a similar weapon.

121. Use a two-handed thrusting blow to block and hit the arm as you kick vigorously into the knee. The blocking action protects you as it stops his intended blow and hurts him.

122. Against a back-handed attack, block the hitting arm from the outside. Be prepared to kick and hit, as necessary.

123. A one-handed block/hit can be used against the back-handed attack in conjunction with a kick.

After stopping the intended blow, which might be enough to stop the attack, be prepared to continue with stick blows and kicks, as necessary to complete the defense and allow you to escape.

121

122

12

124   125

CHAIN ATTACK DEFENSE

The defense used against a chain is also appropriate against any flexible weapon such as belt, rope or rubber hose.

124. The defense used here is only slightly different from the knife defense. Against a flexible weapon, the best defense is directed against the weapon itself. If the weapon is a belt, rope or chain, it will wrap around the stick, giving you the opportunity to kick while immobilizing his attacking weapon.

125. After stopping the intended blow, kick with vigor into his knee or shin. Concentrate all your stick blows at his weapon or weapon hand so that he cannot hit you while you are making your defense.

WHEN TO DEFEND AGAINST KNIFE

Don't risk personal injury in defense of property or money.

It is imprudent and needlessly reckless to attempt a defense against a knife if the intent is not assault, but robbery. Unless you have achieved a high degree of skill, with considerable practice, there is some risk of cutting injury if you defend against an experienced knife man.

If the assault is *not* motivated by robbery, but the intention is to cut you, you have nothing to lose by attempting the defense; on the contrary, you are safer if you make a spirited defense against a cutting assault than if you simply allow yourself to be victimized.

GUN DEFENSE

Only the professional law enforcement officer actually needs to learn defenses against gun threat. For the layman, the prudent and practical procedure is to minimize the danger of being a victim of a gun shooting. Contrary to the common misconception, a high proportion of gun deaths are the result of quarrels, family disputes and accidents. Because most shootings take place out of the range of possible defense, the stick tactics which are effective against attempted knife assault are useless against guns. Those gun defenses which are effective are only practical if they are constantly practiced so that technical skill is maintained.

The ways of minimizing the possibility of being a gun victim are these: Avoid emotional relationships with persons of unstable temperament who own guns. (This is not flippant advice; it is based on the statistics of gun deaths.) If a gun is used to threaten you but the primary motive is robbery, do not resist; your life and health are more important than any material possession.

KNIFE ATTACK DEFENSES

126. The attack is made in a wide, slashing arc; the weapon might be a knife, broken bottle, ice-pick, or other cutting instrument. With a snappy, whipping motion, slash at the wrist or hand. The intent is to hurt his hand or arm as you stop the intended attack. Concentrate all your stick blows at the knife hand and arm, continuing to hit with vigor for as long as necessary to allow you to escape.

127. The attack is a low, straight-in thrust.

128. As the knife hand moves toward you, hit his arm cross-body with a back-handed blow. This will hurt his arm as it deflects the intended attack.

Use vigorous kicks into his shin as you continue to strike his knife hand and arm with snappy, forceful stick blows until you have hurt him enough to allow you to escape.

129. From very close in, against a knife threat which you are fairly certain will develop into action, simultaneous kicking/hitting is the best defense. Divert his attention by making some subtle gesture or sound. You might only have seconds in which to plan your defense, but those seconds are precious if you keep your wits.

126

127

128

129

ROUTINES & PRACTICE PATTERNS

It is characteristic of the traditional forms of Oriental fighting that they present the student with set patterns and routines which must be learned, remembered, practiced and demonstrated in precisely the same sequence as they are taught. Students are not allowed to improvise in the practice or demonstration of the routines. While such prearranged movements have great value for development of technique, they do not permit flexibility of response. In actual street defense, you must be able to react to what is happening, rather than to what you have practiced.

A way of keeping your stick fighting skill at functional level is the practice of long-sequence patterns which you invent yourself. Although constant rigorous training is not necessary for practical defense skill, you should have an occasional review of the techniques to keep them available for emergency use.

The two solo routines which follow are examples of practice patterns. Practice them as shown; use them as models for inventing your own practice routines for review.

SOLO PRACTICE ROUTINE: A

The movements in this routine can be practiced in three distinct styles. The first manner of practice should be smooth, flowing, graceful, continuous actions. When you can perform the routine in this manner, practice it with very slight hesitations between the blows; simulate forceful blows. The third manner of practicing the routine is fast and spirited.

130. Start from a relaxed, standing position; stick point on the floor.

131. Without foot movement, hit up with the point end.

132. Grasp handle end with both hands and draw stick up.

133. Hit into the side.

134. As you side-step, hit into the other side.

135. With a whipping blow, hit as though into the shin.

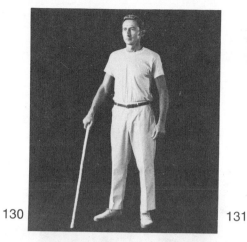

130

131

132

133

134

135

136. Slide your left hand to the point end of the stick and hit around, striking with the handle end.

137. Thrust forward, hitting with the handle.

138. Step forward with your left foot as you bring the point end over and down.

139. Step with your right foot and thrust, as though into the chest, hitting with the middle of the stick.

136

137

138

139

140. Thrust up with the middle of the stick, as though under the chin.

141. Hit down, as though onto the nose, with the middle of the stick.

142. Step back, with your right foot; hold the point of the stick forward.

143. Cue-stick thrusting blow, recoil.

140

141

142

143

144

144. Step back into T-position with your left foot behind you, on guard.

SOLO PRACTICE ROUTINE: B

Begin the practice of this routine slowly, with smooth flowing movements. When you can do it without hesitation, practice it in a fast, spirited manner.

145. Start from ready position, holding stick with both hands, palms down.

146. Block up.

145

146

147

148

147. Step back as you block down, cross-body, as though parry/blocking a kick.

148. Block/deflect cross-body with center of stick, handle end down, as shown.

149. Hitting with the handle end, strike up.

150. Hitting with the point end, hit around.

151. Cue-shot, snappy, with recoil.

152. As you take a step back with your left foot, slide your left hand back to the handle end; gripping the handle end with both hands, strike a whipping blow high, as though into the side of the neck.

149

150

151

152

153. A second whipping blow follows, back-handed, as though into the other side of the neck.

154. A third whipping blow, as though into the side of the leg.

155. A fourth whipping blow as though into the side of the other leg.

156. Step back, on-guard.

153

154

155

156

HAND STICK

The hand stick, also known by the Japanese name of yawara stick, has advantages and disadvantages as a self-defense aid.

The fact that it need not be carried in your hand, as does a cane or umbrella, is both an advantage and a disadvantage, depending on the circumstances.

The major disadvantage of the hand stick is that you must come in closer to apply the defense than is necessary if using a cane or umbrella. For a frail person, the major advantage of the hand stick is that it adds force to a hand blow. The individual who is in normal good health and has normal functional use of his hands, would not ordinarily require a hand stick for defense unless his (or her) work and circumstances exposed him to more than usual danger of assault.

As is true of any stick or weapon, total reliance upon the stick for self-defense presents a danger in itself. If health and body function permit, you should learn weaponless self-defense for practical use and the stick defenses should be considered back-up techniques.

DRAW AND HIT

Unlike the umbrella or walking stick, the hand stick is not normally drawn, ready for use at all times. Unless you expect or apprehend assault or danger, it will not be in your hand, but you should have quick and easy access to it if it is needed. Practice the draw-and-hit procedure as preparation to respond defensively.

Carry the hand stick where *you* can reach it most easily and comfortably. Some individuals find it easier to draw from the front, high (as in the breast pocket of a shirt or jacket); some individuals find it easier to draw from a back pocket (as from the hip pocket of trousers); some individuals can most easily draw the stick from a jacket pocket. It is not convenient for most men to carry or draw from the front trouser pocket. Women can carry the stick in a pocket, or in a handbag which has an open side pouch.

157. At the first indication of assault, draw from the breast pocket and . . .

158 . . . without hesitation, convert the drawing action into a forward blow, striking backhanded. The action is a single movement. The same action would be effective if you were drawing an improvised hand stick from your breast pocket, for instance, pencil, pen or comb.

159. At the first indication of assault, draw from the breast pocket and without hesitation hit to the rear, into the side of the head or neck. Immediately turn to face the assailant.

160. Draw from the breast pocket and hit as though into mid-body area.

157

158

159

160

161

161. At the first indication of assault, draw from the hip or jacket pocket and . . .

162 . . . without hesitation thrust forward into the mid-body area.

163. Draw from the hip or jacket pocket and hit back into the mid-body area. The same draw-and-hit technique would be appropriate if you were drawing an improvised stick such as a pipe, comb or keys.

164, 165. The stick defenses shown for men can be used with equal efficiency by women. Women who are fearful of assault can relieve some of the tension by rehearsal of the correct response to assault situations they fear.

Practice drawing the handstick and having it available for use. Women can make a safety habit of having the stick in hand when walking alone in non-populated, dark areas.

162

163

164

165

ALERT AND ON-GUARD POSITIONS

The totally unexpected, unmotivated, surprise attack is rare. Although you should be able to cope with a surprise attack, the awareness of when attack is imminent is exceedingly important. If you are concerned enough about the possibility of assault or are in a high risk job which justifies carrying of a hand stick for defense, you should take full advantage of the preparedness factor.

There are two main kinds of positions of defense, one is alert and ready without any show of hostility or willingness to fight; the other is frankly on guard.

Alert Positions

The alert positions allow you to negotiate in a possible threatening situation and yet allow you to move into action to defend if you cannot talk your assailant out of physical violence.

Because physical violence is the language of the emotionally unstable, keeping a cool head could help you avoid having to resort to physical defense. If you do not want to be forced into physical conflict, you should be prepared to act as a calming influence. Taunting, threatening, insulting words inflame the emotionally unstable person; low keyed, neutral remarks can help to control him. As you engage in non-hostile conversation, you should be prepared to move into action if he starts to attack.

166. There is a threat of assault, but you judge that you might avoid it. Hold the hand stick concealed to avoid showing willingness to fight. The position shown here is a normal, neutral-looking conversational stance. Create spring tension by pushing forward slightly with the hand holding the stick as you push inward with the hand covering the stick.

167. At the first move to attack, you are ready to hit.

168. This is also a neutral, non-hostile, conversational stance. Your arms are folded, the stick is concealed. Create a spring tension by pushing forward slightly with the hand holding the stick as you push inward with the other arm.

169. If he moves to attack, you can react quickly.

170. With the stick concealed, your arms at your sides, as shown, you can be ready to move if he attacks. Avoid standing in too close. You can keep a safe distance and still maintain a conversational relationship.

171. If he moves, you can react.

166

167

168

169

170

171

On-Guard

The on-guard stance with hand stick displayed is the most protective defensive position. It is for use when the possibility of negotiation does not exist, or has been exhausted, or is negligible. But even in such a situation, you might still avert physical violence by your attitude. Do not threaten your assailant, but make it clear that you are prepared to defend yourself. By the way you talk and by the way your hold yourself you can indicate determination and preparedness.

172. Adversary threatens violence, but is not actually moving to hit. Set yourself in good, strong balance and hold the hand stick out in a defensive gesture.

173. Adversary threatens assault and may be moving in. Set yourself in good balance; display the stick as you assume a guard stance with one hand held high and the other low. You are ready to deliver simultaneous blows from this position.

174. For those individuals who are more comfortable using the standard boxing fighting stance, this is a good guard. Display the stick in one hand and hold the other hand fisted.

175. A variation of the standard boxing stance is with your lead hand holding the stick.

Any of the above guard stances can be used, according to individual preference.

172

173

174

175

ONE-HANDED REACH

Because so many aggressive actions begin with a reaching gesture, you should be prepared to cope with it before it has become a completed action. You do not have to wait to find out whether he intends to push, pull, grab, or poke — you respond to the reaching out and stop the intended action.

176

176. As the arm comes forward, strike down onto the wrist, hand or forearm. Avoid stepping toward the assailant to hit the reaching arm. Practice hitting at the hand or wrist as your first choice.

177

177. Another possible response is to block/parry the reaching arm with a forearm blow, ready to hit with the stick, if necessary. Very often, stopping the first intended action of an assault is enough to deter an assailant.

178

179

178. Hit the reaching arm with the stick and follow through . . .

179 . . . with a second stick blow and kick, if necessary.

180

180. Or, you can use a forearm blow to deflect the intended action as you hit with the stick and kick. If the situation is serious, the triple action is the most appropriate and effective.

TWO-HANDED REACH

181. The response to two hands reaching is similar to the defense against one-handed reaching; you should practice to cope with both reaching hands. Step to the side of the assailant and hit down onto one of the reaching arms.

182. Hit one reaching arm with the stick as you parry/block the other arm with your forearm.

183. Hit one arm with the stick as you parry the other arm and kick. The triple, simultaneous actions are the most effective.

181

182

183

GRABBING

Although you should practice to stop or deflect the reaching arm before the action is completed, you should also be prepared to cope with the grab after it has been taken. There is a wide range of possible seriousness in this situation; it could be anything from an angry gesture without intent to hurt you or it could be the first action of a serious assault. You can tell the difference. Respond in the appropriate manner.

184. Against a minor threat, hit into the elbow with enough force to hurt his arm, bending his elbow. Be prepared to continue.

185. Against a more serious threat of assault, hit with force onto the arm as you kick vigorously into the shin, continuing as required by the situation.

186. Against a two-handed grab, hit one arm with the stick and slash at the other arm.

184

185

186

WRIST GRABS

With proper preventive procedures, it is unlikely that you would find yourself in this situation, but being prepared to cope with it is useful for confidence.

187. Your wrists are grabbed, presumably by a considerably stronger person. Kick with vigor into his shins, continuing until you have hurt him enough to loosen his grip somewhat.

188. Snap one hand free by using a quick, twisting action, effecting release at the weak part of his grip, between his thumb and forefinger. Draw the stick.

189. Hit at the shoulder muscle of his free hand.

190. Hit onto the back of his gripping hand. Continue hitting and kicking as necessary for release.

187

188

189

190

FRONT CHOKE

The defense against a front choke is similar to the response to
front grab; your blows must be vigorous and snappy. Release of
the choking pressure is the essential first action.

191. Strike into the bend of both elbows, with vigor and snap, as
you kick into the shin. Concentrate your main effort against his
elbows to relieve the choking pressure. Continue to hit as necessary to effect release.

192. Hitting onto the shoulder muscle weakens his arm and may
immobilize it. Alternate hitting at his elbow and his shoulder with
the stick.

191

192

193

193. Or, you can hit onto the
top of the nose. Hitting onto
the nose requires greater precision than hitting the shoulder
muscle, but it is an effective
blow. Hit and kick as necessary
to allow you to escape.

FIST ATTACK

Stay as far out of fist range of your adversary as is possible in the situation. Even when you are in close quarters, maintain the maximum distance permitted by the space.

194. If you have room in which to maneuver, step or dodge to the outside of the punching arm as you block/parry and kick into his leg.

195. Follow with a stick blow into his arm or onto the shoulder muscle. It is advantageous to keep moving and to move around to the rear of your assailant if you can.

196. If there is less space in which to maneuver and you are in closer to the assailant, block/parry the punching arm upward and . . .

194

195

196

197 . . . be prepared to block/slash the other arm as you kick into the shin . . .

198 . . . and follow with a stick blow onto the shoulder muscle or his forearm. Continue hitting and kicking as necessary to complete your defense.

199. You can block/parry both his arms as you kick into the shin . . .

200 . . . and without hesitation follow with stick blows as necessary to complete the defense.

197

198

199

200

IMPROVISING HAND STICKS

Men and women ordinarily carry common objects which can be used as sticks.   Men can use a pen, a comb, a pocket knife (closed) or keys as self-defense aids, using them in the same fashion as a hand stick. Women can carry a hand stick in an open pouch of a hand bag, or can utilize comb, brush, keys, pen, purse mirror or similar objects as hand sticks. A rolled-up magazine or newspaper or a book can be used as a hand stick.

Flashlight as Hand Stick

A flashlight is a useful object for an improvised hand stick. You should have a flashlight in your car. You would do well to get into the habit of carrying a flashlight when walking from the car to the house at night and when walking alone in dark areas, getting into elevators, etc. Shop keepers, nightworkers and guards usually have a flashlight handy. Without giving the appearance of hostility or nervousness, you can carry a flashlight, ready to use as a hand stick for defense.

SEATED

Women are more likely to be annoyed or threatened from a seated position than men. Practice hand stick and improvised hand stick defenses appropriate to the annoying situation and to more serious danger.

201. Against a merely annoying individual, a moderate blow down onto the hand would be enough to deter.

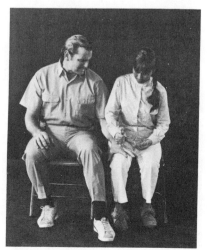

201

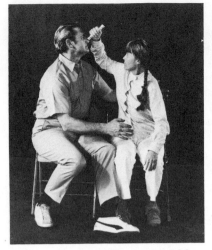 

202   203

202. Against a more serious assault, hitting onto the nose would be appropriate and effective.

203. Hitting up under the jaw and stamping down onto the instep could be followed by additional stick blows into the side of the neck and down onto the forearm.

DEFENSE AGAINST KICKS

It is difficult and inefficient to try to grip, grapple with or block a kick with your hands or arms. The leg is considerably stronger than the arm. You put yourself in danger of being kicked in the face or groin if you attempt to deal with a kicking attack using your hands. Parry/blocking or deflecting a kick is more efficient and safer. As you parry/block, move your hips back, as shown in the photos.

204. Against a knee kick, use a vigorous stick blow to deflect the kicking leg. Hit at the knee for best effect.

205. Against a toe kick or heel stamp, deflect the leg as close to the ankle as possible. Use the stick for hitting, but if you miss the target with the stick, you can deflect efficiently with your forearm.

206. A moderately forceful deflecting blow will turn him away from you and you can continue by hitting down onto the shoulder muscle and kicking into the back of his knee, if necessary.

A very low kick should be blocked with your foot. Do not bend over to try to block a low kick; bending over makes you vulnerable to attack.

204

205

206

OVER-ARM PIN

Like the grabbing attack, this is a situation which could be avoided by using precautionary tactics. Knowing how to cope with it will give you confidence.

207. You are caught in a surprise attack, your arms pinned. Kick with vigor into his shin, scrape down his shin and stamp onto his instep; repeat until you feel his grip is somewhat loosened to allow you to . . .

208 . . . clasp your hands together (do not intertwine your fingers) and take a deep breath to expand his grip further. Exhale suddenly and squat down to effect release.

209. Hit into his mid-section with your elbow. Draw the stick.

210. Immediately turn to face him, ready to hit and kick, if necessary.

The same defense is effective for similar situations — under-arm body grab, arm pin, rear wrist grips, etc.

207

208

209

210

BACK CHOKE

The essential element of this defense is stopping the choking pain; unless you stop the pressure of the choke *first,* you are in danger of losing consciousness. Begin your defense before you draw the stick.

211. Back choke is effected, pressure is applied with the forearm. *First* grip his choking arm at the wrist and take a firm hold; jerk down on his arm and turn your head into the bend of his elbow; kick with force into his shin. These actions will not break the choke hold but they will give you some relief from the pressure. Now draw the stick.

212. Hit up and back into his face . . .

213 . . . or down and back into his body. Continue kicking and hitting with the stick while you maintain a firm hold on his choking arm. When you have hurt him enough that you feel his grip is loosened . . .

214 . . . duck down and step back to escape.

211

212

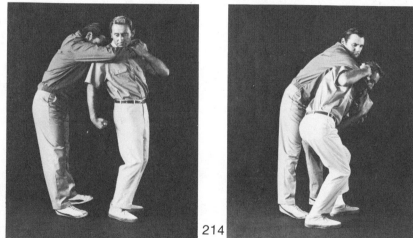

213

214

DEFENSE AGAINST BLUDGEON/CLUB

Because a bludgeon or club extends the hitting range of your assailant, it is safer to move in for the defense. This is one of the few instances in which you deliberately move toward your assailant.

Back-Hand Attack

215. Against a back-handed club (or tire-iron or other rigid striking weapon) duck to the outside of the hitting arm and parry/block it with stick and slashing blows.

216. While you are delivering stick blows to his shoulder muscle and the side of his neck, immobilize his weapon arm by maintaining pressure with your other hand, and kick into his leg. Continue as necessary to complete the defense.

Wide Swinging Attack

217. The wide swinging attack is clearly indicated by the way he extends the club.

218. Block/parry the hitting arm at his wrist and forearm.

219. Immobilize his hitting arm by keeping your forearm in place, as you hit onto the shoulder muscle with the stick. Continue with stick and foot blows as required to complete the defense.

215

216

217

218

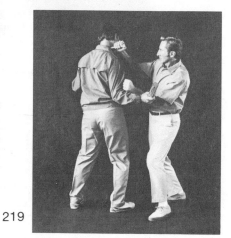

219

220   221

Jabbing Thrust

220. Against a straight thrust in with a rigid weapon, step to the outside of the hitting arm and block/parry it with your forearm.

221. Place your hand at his arm and maintain pressure to immobilize, as you hit down onto his arm or shoulder muscle. Continue as necessary.

KNIFE ATTACK

Unless you are in danger of being cut, your most prudent action is calm cooperation. The defense attempt should only be made in the same kinds of circumstances outlined in the cane/umbrella section. Reread that material before you practice the hand stick defense against knife threat and knife attack.

Close-In Threat

222. If you have no alternative except to defend yourself, begin the defense with a subtle distraction. Do *not* try to draw the stick *first*.

223. Thrust his knife hand cross-body and keep your arm extended and rigid to allow a few seconds in which to continue without danger of being cut. Without hesitation, thrusting finger stabs into his eyes.

224. As you draw the stick, kick with vigor into his leg.

225. Hit his knife hand at the wrist or onto the back of his hand. Do *not* attempt to grapple or wrest the knife away; continue stick blows and kicks as necessary to hurt or subdue him and allow you to escape.

222

223

224

225

Moving-In Knife Attack

In this situation, the attack is in progress; he is moving forward and threatening with the knife. Do not move in toward him.

226. As he comes toward you, take a long step out to the side of his knife hand; this places you in the best position from which to defend.

227. With your arm extended and rigid, lock his knife arm away from you; kick with vigor into his leg or the back of his knee.

228. Maintaining your grip on his knife arm, hit with the stick into the side of the neck, onto the shoulder muscle, onto his knife hand. Do *not* attempt to grip or grapple with the knife; do not attempt to wrest it away from him. Concentrate on hurting him sufficiently to allow you to escape. A vigorous kick into the knee could buckle him down or put him on the ground.

226

227

228

SPECIAL OFFICERS

Guards and special officers have two main types of functions and duties; protection of property and prevention of disturbances at public gatherings. The two duties are dissimilar and require different approaches, tactics and handling.

Those duties of private and special officers which most resemble police work should be prepared for by training and instruction which is appropriate to those duties. It is not within the scope of this book to present the instruction which is intended for police and police-type duties. Professionals in law enforcement will find the techniques of defense and control, including baton tactics, in DEFENSE TACTICS FOR LAW ENFORCEMENT.*

The special officer who is permitted to carry a hand stick or a baton can use them for self-defense in much the same manner as is shown in the cane section and in the hand stick section.

BATON TACTICS: STOPPING FIGHTS

The baton has advantages over the hand stick for stopping fights and separating disputants. The baton can be used for holding-off actions, it can be used as a bumper and it can be used without coming in very close. The baton has more preventive uses than the hand stick and it has, properly used, greater effectiveness. Because the baton or night stick has been crudely used, as a bludgeon, it has a reputation in some quarters as being solely an offensive weapon. It need not be; it can be used intelligently and effectively for prevention and protection.

229

230

*Thor Publishing Company, Ventura, California 1972

229. Staying out of fist range of the aggressor, you can nudge him away with a pushing movement of the baton. If it is necessary, a jabbing action into the mid-body can be used. With the holding-off action, use a verbal command to the second person to leave. If necessary, use your free hand to block him.

230. The baton can also be used one-handed for shoving, using the point.

231. Or, held alongside your arm, the full length can be used.

232. Both ends can be used to separate two aggressive individuals.

233. A two-handed grip can be used for pushing the aggressive person from the front . . .

234 . . . from the side . . .

231

232

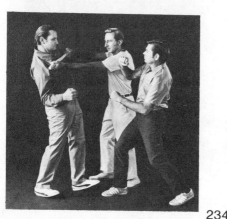
233

234

235 . . . or back.

It is not wise to come in between two persons fighting, and you should stay out of fist range, if possible.

If one of the disputants is clearly the victim and the other is clearly the aggressor, begin the action by working against the aggressor.

236. If it is necessary to remove the aggressive individual, you can use the point end of the baton to push him as you walk.

237. Or, you can use the stick as a lever to assist the walking away.

238. If the fight cannot be stopped simply by separating the individuals, there are a few simple techniques which can be used for immobilizing and hurting the aggressor without using brutal tactics. An effective tactic for stopping a fist fight is striking down onto the hand, wrist or forearm . . .

239 . . . and immediately hitting into the shin.

240. If you are behind the two men, you can hit down onto the shoulder muscle . . .

241 . . . or into the back of the knee . . .

242 . . . or into the side of the knee.

235

236

237

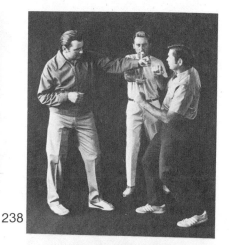

238

239

240

241

242

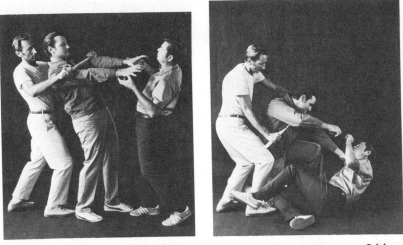

243   244

243. If necessary, you could then use the baton to pull back against the chest and separate.

244. If the fight is on the ground, the baton can be used as a lever to pull one man away from the other.

Whenever possible, avoid coming in between the disputants.

HAND STICK: STOPPING FIGHTS

The advantage of the hand stick is that it may be carried concealed and that even when it is carried in your hand it is not an obvious weapon. The disadvantage of the hand stick is that you must come in close to the assailant to use it and that it is less useful than the baton as a separating instrument. The hand stick is primarily useful for adding force to blows, but it can be used for nudging. When it is properly used — avoiding the high-risk-of-injury target areas — it is effective without being brutal.

245. The hand stick can be used to nudge into the neck as you give verbal instructions to separate. While this action is moderate, it is persuasive.

246. You can hit at the wrist or forearm to stop a fight in progress.

247. You can hit down onto the shoulder muscle from the rear.

245

246

247

248   249

248. If necessary, hand stick blows can be utilized to stop a fight in progress, alternating blows at both disputants.

249. If one of the men is clearly the victim and the other the aggressor, the stick can be used to help you separate the men. Push into the mid-section with the stick as you pull back under his chin.

CONTROL AND SELF-CONTROL

A quiet air of authority, being in control without giving the impression of hostility or apprehension, is essential to non-physical control of group action and movement. Many of the events which attract large crowds also generate a good deal of emotion, some of which may be exuberant good spirits and some may be anger and frustration. Do not expect the crowd to be courteous to you; you are paid to be courteous to them.

Clearly, the performance of the duty of keeping order at a public function involves a high degree of self-control and a disinterested attitude. The special officer who is hired to help keep the peace is expected to behave himself as though he were a neutral party, not a disputant in a dispute.

The businessman who uses special officers to prevent disturbances at a sporting event does not want his customers treated as though they were criminals. Though a crowd might become excited and unruly, though some of them might get drunk and pugnacious, they are expected to be treated as though they were customers.

A good officer uses tact and persuasion to handle potential disturbances. He can spot trouble before it gets to the fighting stage. He is able to guide, to warn without threatening, to calm excitement — in other words, to contribute a cooling effect. This skill is a function of experience, character and personality. It is also a function of confidence; the officer who knows he can handle a fight in progress has the poise which will help him prevent disturbances.

BATON: CONTROLLING CROWD FLOW

A crowd which is in high spirits may, nonetheless, become aggressive if it is irritated or provoked. There is a tendency to confuse caution with surliness. It is necessary and important that you maintain *caution* and a *pleasant demeanor* when you are working crowd flow.

At most of the gatherings for which special officers are used, there is not the preparation, leadership or sufficient personnel to control an active disturbance. Your important function is prevention and avoidance. If, in such a situation, you use the baton as a hitting weapon, you are more likely to aggravate the situation than control it. The baton must only be used as a bumper-shield, as protection and as a barrier.

To guide crowd flow, the baton is used to *press* (not hit) toward the area where there is adequate exit. You must not try to keep the people in front of a crowd from moving; if you do that, they are forced forward by pressure from the back of the crowd. An injury inflicted on someone at this point could turn an excited crowd into an angry mob.

Should a crowd turn angry or violent, there is no effective way in which you can function except to prevent injury and damage as much as is possible. For your own personal safety, as well as for the interests of your employer you must not punish (by hurting) individuals in a rowdy crowd. Even though they are rowdy, the businessman wants them back for his next paying event. It is assumed that when a situation gets out of hand, reinforcements will be called in.

If you have any questions about regulations governing the use of stick weapons for your job, it is your responsibility to find out about them. Under the law, you are responsible for your actions and ignorance of the law is no defense in court.

DEFENSES FOR THE BLIND

Instructing the Blind

This book is organized for home-study by students who do not have instructor assistance, but because he cannot correlate the written text with the photos, the blind student will need teaching help. The material which follows is intended for the individual who is not experienced in teaching a physical skill to a blind person.

Instructors who are familiar with teaching the blind may adapt the material to suit their own teaching methods.

The Concept

Before you begin teaching self-defense to a blind student, you must communicate this critical concept: Learning self-defense is not a matter of becoming an expert fighter, it is a matter of learning a few practical, simple, effective tactics. The person who assaults a blind person expects no orderly defense. The person who assaults a blind person is a coward. Cowards only assault those whom they expect to be helpless victims. To counter the assault of a coward, it is necessary to avoid the role of helpless victim, by responding in an orderly, effective, spirited manner.

WHICH TECHNIQUES FOR THE BLIND?

The actual defenses which are useful for the blind are the same as those which are taught in the cane, umbrella and walking stick section and in the hand stick section. The blind student need not learn all of the defenses in those sections, but should practice them all in order to select those which seem comfortable and possible for him to learn and use. Some students are satisfied to learn only a few tactics which they can use with ease, others are made more confident by practicing a greater variety of techniques. As a general rule, it is better to know a smaller group of techniques very well than it is to learn the maximum number of techniques.

SUGGESTED PROCEDURE

The teacher should read the entire book and glance at all the photos. You should be familiar with all the material before you begin helping your blind student. Next, you should read all of the appropriate material aloud to your student. He should be familiar with the concepts and general information before he begins to practice.

PRACTICING THE TECHNIQUES

Read the instruction aloud. The student will then perform the technique as you have described it, in solo practice so that you can watch his actions. Compare his gesture and action with the photo which illustrates the technique. A high level of technical proficiency is not necessary for basic defense; his performance should correspond, in general, to the technique as it is shown in the photo. Correct only those errors which clearly invalidate the intent of the technique.

Because the blind student must memorize everything he learns, work slowly, do not rush through the material. A few short sessions of defense are preferable to one long session of instruction and practice.

Avoid handling your student whenever possible. Give your instructions verbally and make corrections verbally.

Because the blind student is accustomed to learning by touch, allow him to touch you so that he can "feel" the correct technique, gesture and action.

Make your corrections in a positive way, rather than in a negative manner. If, for instance, you ask him to simulate hitting at knee level and he does it incorrectly, avoid saying "that's wrong," instead, tell him what he *is* to do; "aim higher" or "aim lower" are positive corrections.

Because the blind depend on hearing to orient to distance and position, it is best to work in a room which is not heavily carpeted.

Rely on your student's responses to help you help him. Every group which has special problems to cope with is a source of inventive and practical solutions for those problems. As is true of every other special group I have ever worked with (policemen, stunt men, the orthopedically disabled) the blind were my instructors at the same time that they were my students.

Encourage

Blind students learn self-defense very well. During the many years when I had a school of self-defense in Hollywood, no single group of students gave me greater satisfaction to teach than did the blind. Like any other student, the blind student may have reservations about accepting new ideas, but once the concept is accepted, he can learn this relatively simple skill. You can motivate your student by telling him that the author has taught self-defense to blind students with a high degree of success. Your patient help and encouragement are essential factors in promoting confidence in your student.

ADAPTING THE MATERIAL

With your student's help, you will make necessary adaptations of the material as you proceed through the text. Different individuals will require a different degree of adaptation. There is as great a range of learning capacity and learning problems among the blind as there is among sighted students. Much of the material, the various grips and methods of striking, for instance, will be practiced by the blind student exactly as practiced by the sighted student. The major adaptation for blind students will be where to strike. Instead of learning specific body targets, blind students will practice three levels at which to strike: head level, mid-body level and leg level.

After practicing the ways of holding and hitting, begin practice of striking at the three levels. Use sound cues to indicate that the blow should be delivered high (at head level), in the mid-body area, or low (at leg level). At first, make your sound cues obvious and easy to follow. With practice, your student should develop the ability to strike into any of the three areas when given more subtle clues. You can snap your fingers or clap your hands to indicate the target level.

250. On the appropriate sound cue, hit high, as though into the side of the neck or head.

251. Practice striking into the area of the knee or shin.

252. Hit into the mid-body area.

When hitting into these three general areas, perfect precision is not needed; a fair degree of accuracy is sufficient.

MAKING CONTACT

For the blind student, even more than for the sighted student, it is useful to have the practice of making contact blows. The blind student can only *feel* when he has performed a technique correctly. Unlike the sighted student, he does not have the visual evidence of coming close to the "assailant" in practice. Follow the safety rules carefully. With the cane, light blows can be very painful. For full-force contact blows, use the cardboard box or improvise objects which the student can hit vigorously taking every precaution to make sure that you do not get hit; a full-force blow can be more than painful; it can cause injury.

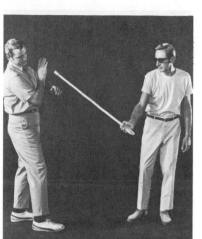

250

251

252

TRAINING AIDS

To allow your student to practice contact blows with his cane, you can improvise an object which he can hit without danger of hurting you. Making contact blows is a useful procedure and the blows should be executed with vigor and spirit.

253   254

253. A cardboard carton makes an ideal striking target; it is light enough to hold in various positions and it can be hit hard. Practice one-handed downward blows, as shown. Turn the "target" side of the box so that he can hit back-handed swinging blows at it without danger of hitting your hands. Practice all the one-handed grip blows.

254. Practice the two-handed grip blows, the jabbing blow as shown, and the other two-handed blows.

GUIDE DOGS

If your student has a guide dog, the dog should be integrated into the self-defense training. The dog should be present during practice sessions. Particular care should be taken to make sure that the dog does not misinterpret the defensive use of the cane. A dog which has not been trained for protection, but for obedience and guidance, may react with fear unless it is prepared to recognize this special use.

DEFENSES FOR THE DISABLED

Self-defense for the orthopedically disabled person will vary with the specific degree and type of disability. The ability to learn self-defense will vary also with the degree to which the disabled person thinks of himself (or herself) as "handicapped" or helpless as opposed to competent but limited in physical activity. There is no point in denying that the orthopedically disabled person is likely to be more vulnerable to assault than others, but it is non-productive to stress that fact.

When the concept of helplessness is fostered, it leads to a further degree of helplessness and vulnerability; when the possibility of competence is emphasized, it promotes a feeling of confidence and well-being.

An individual who assaults a disabled person is not expecting a fight nor is he expecting an orderly defense; he expects a helpless victim.

The disabled person who reacts to the threat of assault with a spirited, orderly defense, even when his tactics are limited, is less likely to be hurt than is the individual who presents himself in the role of helpless victim.

WHAT CAN YOU LEARN?

The defenses which are shown in this section are given as examples for the disabled student. You should study all the cane, umbrella, and hand stick defense shown in the text and select those which are possible for you to do. Because your ability is limited, work to develop a higher level of skill at the techniques you can perform as a way of overcoming the limitations.

Emphasize those techniques which you can use with confidence. Remember that a relatively small repertoire of effective defense tactics takes you out of the category of "helpless." Knowing only two or three useful defense actions could make the difference between having to act the passive victim and being able to take care of yourself.

HAND & FOOT BLOWS

Practice all of the hand and foot blows which you can do. Make use of your functioning limbs to the greatest degree possible. If you can kick with one leg, practice kicking with that leg; if you can use your legs, but not your hands, emphasize practice of kicking blows. If your disability limits the use of your legs but allows you the use of your arms, emphasize practice of the hand blows. As much as possible, avoid total dependence on the stick as your weapon of self-defense.

STANDING BALANCE

If you use a cane, get into the habit of using it for strong balance.

255. You can practice kicking as you support your weaker side with the cane. Especially if you are considerably stronger on one side than the other, practice this method of kicking. Practice the out-of-fist range kick, as shown.

256. Practice the close-in kicks in the same manner.

257. Using the cane to give you three-point balance, practice the various hand blows. Slash onto the forearm or into the bend of the elbow.

258. Practice the hand blows in the manner which is appropriate to your specific condition. Support your weaker side with the cane; slash into both sides of the neck with the open-hand blow.

259. Striking onto the nose with the side of the fist is an easy and effective defense action.

260. A thrusting, heel-of-palm blow up under the chin can be used effectively close in.

255

256

257

258

259

260

SEATED DEFENSE

From a wheelchair, or seated, concentrate on hand blows, practice all the stick defenses which are possible for you to do. Avoid complete dependence on the stick or cane.

261. Hit down onto the reaching arm with the hand stick. Practice, also, hitting down onto the reaching arm with a slashing open-hand blow or strike the arm with your forearm. You do not have to wait until the attack is completed to begin your defense; react to the aggressive, reaching action.

262. Hit up and away with the hand stick. Practice striking upward at the reaching arm, using a choppy, slashing open-hand blow.

263. Practice simultaneous blows, using stick and hand blows at the same time. Shown is a hand stick blow into the side of the neck as the other hand is using for a slapping, heel-of palm parry.

Practice a variety of hand and stick blows, hitting into the target areas which are presented to you in the seated position.

DEFENSE FROM THE GROUND

If you are pushed down or fall, do not try to get up, but carry on your defense from the ground. You are at a disadvantage and vulnerable if you try to rise.

264. Use crutch or cane to hit jabbing blows into the mid-section or face. Continue until safe to rise.

265. Hit into the leg or knee, continuing as necessary to allow you to rise in safety. A short arc allows you to hit a fast sequence of forceful blows with the butt end of the stick.

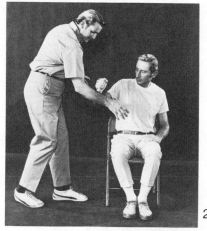

261

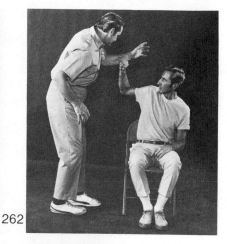

262

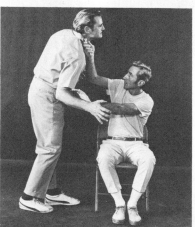

263

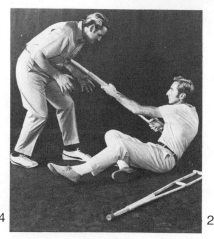

264

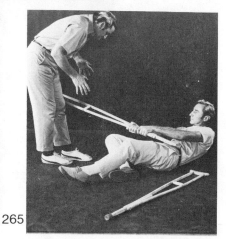

265

CRUTCHES FOR BALANCE & STRIKING

Practice using your crutches in the most effective way for maintaining balance and striking defensive blows.

266. Support your weaker side with a crutch as you deliver a jabbing forward blow with the end of the other crutch.

267. Support yourself with one stick as you hit with the butt end of the other, striking into the side of the head or neck.

268. As you support yourself with one stick, use a raking back-and-forth motion, with vigor.

269. The same raking action can be used for hitting into the legs; or you can use a whipping slash into the knee.

270. Do not step in any closer than you need to to begin your defense. If you are already close in, you can hit upward under the chin, as shown.

271. You can also use the stick for jabbing down onto the top of the foot, using a series of quick, forceful jabs.

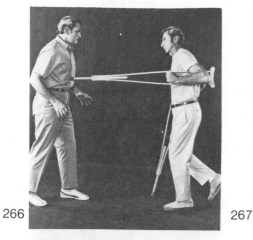

266

267

268

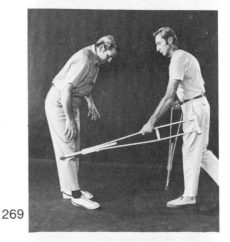

269

270

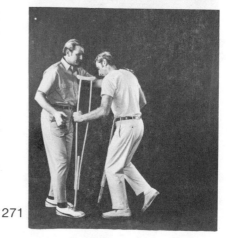

271

CANE BLOWS, TWO-HANDED

From the wheelchair, or seated position, practice cane and umbrella blows.

272. Gripping the cane with both hands, strike at the reaching arm with a whipping action.

273. Hit into the side of the neck . . .

274 . . . and immediately follow the first blow with a second one into the other side of the neck.

275. Use the cane for a straight-in jabbing thrust.

272

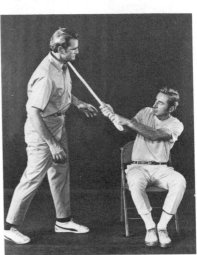

273

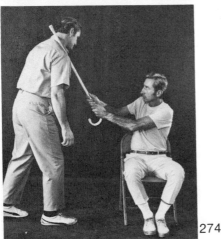

274

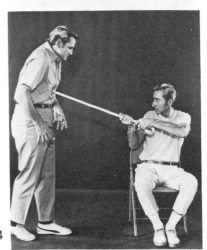

275

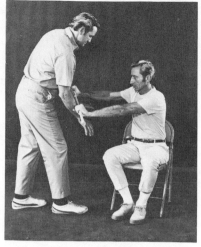
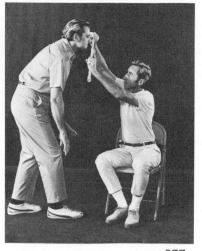

276

277

276. To block and hit, grip the cane with one hand at each end and strike downward at the reaching arms.

277. Without hesitation, follow the blocking blow with an upward blow into the face or up under the chin.

DISTRACTION

278. Any object thrown at the assailant can help your defense. Even a handkerchief is useful for the purpose of diverting his attention from the aggressive act. As you throw the object to distract, hit with force using a one-handed grip on the stick.

278

INDEX

BRUCE TEGNER books are available at bookstores and magazine stands throughout the world. If your local dealer does not stock the title you want, it can be ordered for you, or you may order directly from the publisher. For a free descriptive borchure write:

THOR BOOKS
P O BOX 1782
VENTURA, CA 93001